SOUL JOURNEY

A Poetic Testament of Life, Death, and Life Restored

Tronotia L. Balka

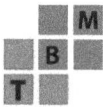

TB Ministries
Your Prophetic Destiny is at Hand!

Soul Journey

A Poetic Testament of Life, Death, and Life Renewed

Tronotia L. Balka

Published in the United States by Tronotia L. Balka and Lawson Media Services.

www.tbministries.net
www.lawsonmediaservices.com

Lawson Media Services
ONLINE SOLUTIONS FOR BUSINESS SUCCESS

ISBN: **0692324062**
ISBN-13 **978-0692324066**:

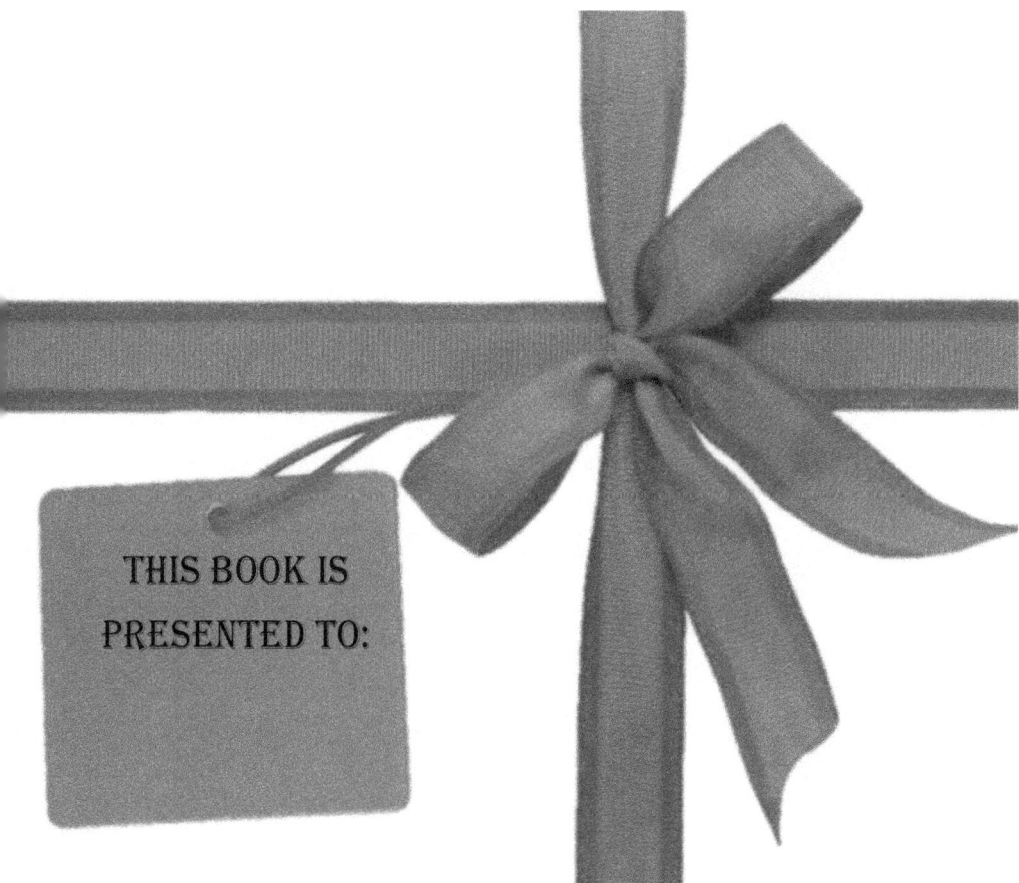

THIS BOOK IS

PRESENTED TO:

DEDICATION

This book is dedicated to all those who love me, and have helped and assisted me through one of the darkest times of my life. I thank you, I love you, and I appreciate you!

A special thanks to my family:

My son Roy
My parents Rev. Davis & Nellie Malveauex
My sisters Tyla & Tacia
My brother Darwin
and all of my nieces and nephews

Last, but certainly not least, I dare not go without giving honor and reverence to my Lord and Savior, Jesus Christ. I am so eternally grateful to have been *gifted* the opportunity to get a glimpse into your "perfect kingdom" for. Now, I know that you have a purpose and a plan for me here on this Earth, and I will see you at the appointed time. I love you.

Amen

ADDITIONAL RESOURCES

Dear *Soul Journey* Readers:

As a thank you for picking up a copy of the book, I'd like to invite you to visit my website at http://tbministries.net/ for free resources and ministry insight to assist you along your journey.

Also by Tronotia Balka

10 Hours Later (Fall 2014)
A Prophets Prayer Journal (Spring 2015)
The Power of Me (Fall 2014)

PREFACE

Soul Journey is a compilation of poems that was written to verbally express my innermost emotions during one of the darkest hours of my existence.

After 10 hours of brain surgery left me blind, deaf, mute, and paralyzed, I endured extensive therapy for months. It was then that I began to reflect on my life and all that God had done for me. Once I was finally able to legibly write, I felt the need to express myself through poetry. I am so grateful to now share with you my thoughts during that dark, yet enlightening, time.

This book is intended to inspire, motivate, and evoke praise unto God, the Most High—my healer and deliverer. Even when my doctors had given up hope, God sustained me and performed a great testimony, due to which I am alive to tell the world my story today.

This book is a great gift of encouragement and testament for people of all religious backgrounds. The God I serve allowed me the gift of life, and I believe He wants to entreat you and fill your life with the same gift. Be sure to read the conclusion at the end of this book to learn more of what His gift is.

Thank you

TABLE OF CONTENTS

DEDICATION...v

Additional Resources..vii

Preface..ix

Table of Contents...xi

Born...3

Dream...5

Ready Or Not...6

Still I Rise...9

A Word..12

Zion Calls...14

Chosen...17

Love..18

The Sound Of Love..19

Baby Boy...21

As A Mother...24

TABLE OF CONTENTS [CON'T]

Time 26

As The Sun Sets..27

Changes...28

Feelings 31

Free...33

As I Lay...36

But I'm Still Here..40

Ability 42

Survivor...45

This Time 47

Thanks...48

Conclusion: His Gift..50

About the Author...53

Need a Ministry Speaker?...55

Stay in touch..57

Don't Forget...Resources 59

The
SOUL JOURNEY
BEGINS...

Born

Why was I born?
I was born to write;
born to sing;
born to give praise to God.
I was born to be me.

In this life I may laugh or I may cry,
but one things for sure—I will live, and not die,
enjoying each day as a gift and a privilege,
knowing that my life had a tragic dilemma.

Born to be free, not anyone's slave.
Success, whatever my trade.
Reaching to others a helping hand.
Shouldn't we want others to make it to their promised land?

Not pulling and fighting to hold you back,
but pushing you forward to make it to the top.
So are you here on this planet called Earth—
just to be mortal, sophisticated dirt?

Make it count,
the life you have been given.
Leave your mark, think of your children.

Suddenly they'll have the right to say,
"My parents paved the way."
Don't waste your time on nonsense and game.
discover your purpose; do it today.

Then you will answer
the question I posed at first.
The reason why you were born—
To be a blessing and not a curse.

Tronotia L. Balka

DREAM

We dream and aspire something as we grow.
Will our childhood fantasies come true? We don't know.

Some say a fireman is what I dream of becoming;
Others say a policeman is what I am seeing.

A little girl looks in the mirror and says,
"I will be a princess one day, I can feel it."

But as dreams appear and life is altered
we learn to take steps forward.

Turning dreams from thoughts to reality,
no longer a childhood fantasy.

A dream realized.
A precious prize.

READY OR NOT

To be tested and tried is the way God conforms us,
       for levels, dimensions, and promotions
       are given to those He trusts.

To go through our toughest trials with faith in God is a must.
       To allow the word of God to have legs and be
       walked out in our lives is how God witnesses
       through us.

But, are you ready?

Do you have your shield of faith ready for battle,
       or, are you still hiding in the shadows?

Are you prepared with the gospel of peace
       for when the enemy comes in like a thief?

Do you have the word hidden in your heart
       just in case from your Bible you depart?

Are you ready for the real deal of Christianity,
        not just lifting your hands singing
        pretending to be?

You see, when "Yes" falls from your lips
        make sure in your heart "Yes" exists.

Your "Yes" must have stability
        and not cower in the face of your enemy.

Are you ready?

Your "Yes" must be able to stand the test of time;
        a total surrender gives Him authority
        to say "You are mine."

At any time, trials may come and
        have the ability to knock you down,
        but don't turn your smile into a frown.

Well ready or not, here He comes,
        the One whose hand you must not let go of.

Anything he brings you to,
        remember, He will bring you through.

Never allow the fear of the unknown
        to hinder you.

God is with you; God is for you;
        He will stand against whatever forms.
        Make sure you are ready for whatever comes.

Are you ready?

STILL I RISE

In life we all have moments of disbelief,
undeniable pain,
and relentless shame.

We will all have to endure the times
of drought;
this is without a doubt.

Whether emotional turmoil looms overhead
or financial burdens try
and stop you instead.

One attitude
we must all remember
is that of a winner who trudges on—
January through December.

Still, I will rise!

No matter how low life has weighed you down, or how high
it seems 'till your breakthrough, you must climb.
Make up your mind.

Many still
don't believe
that there is an enemy
that is determined to knock us to our knees.

If by chance he does succeed,
pray a prayer while on your knees,
As you begin to stand
up straight and lift your hands.
Say loudly,
and say it proudly.

Still, I will rise!

Rise from disappointment.
Rise from defeat.
Rise from retreat.

Still, I will rise!

Rise from disaster.
Rise from sickness.
Rise from sadness.

Still, I will rise!

Into a place of joy and happiness.
Yes, no matter how it looks
like pages in a book.

I turn my chapter
to the place of laughter.

A Word

Have you ever needed to hear just one word from The Boss;
a word that would bring peace to your chaos?

Calm your storm and allow deliverance to start;
see a brighter future and bring love to your heart?

A word that could take the stumble out of your step
and put swagger back in your motion…a word that will help?

A word to bring all the negative issues that surround you to a
  complete halt;
To give a bit of solace to contain your thoughts?

A word to bring still your raging sea;
a word to clear your eyes and enable you to see?

Just one word to help you see a clearer view;
Lord, today let that word come from you.

We've heard from people and given ear to their advice.
When it's over, we still need to see the light.

A word of direction from above.
A word of deliverance that some have yet heard of.

No more warmed-over words or
    something repeated from T.V. shows,
but a fresh word from the Lord,
    is what we need for our souls.

Our spirits are clear;
speak on today God… a word we are so desperate to hear.

ZION CALLS

A nation awaits the voice of one that has been called by God.
To bring the good news of the gospel of peace and proclaim
  to the world that Jesus is on their side.

A nation is now looking for the voice that has the word of
  deliverance they need.
But, as they wait, the question asked is: "Who is the one they
  await for to tell them about the One that did bleed?"

Is it you?

Who will cause the gospel to reach and be
  preached in the remote areas of the world?

Is it you?

That will cause God's word to be heard
so that others will believe and begin to serve?

One person to hear God's truth,
can tell another and that makes two.

But if your voice is never heard,
and in silence you keep God's word;

Those who await you may never know the price
    that Jesus paid.
So whether one or a million,
    make sure your voice has said…

Jesus hung and bled for your sins
    to be forgiven with tears,
He cried then He died;
    to give you peace as you live out your lives.

Is it you?

That will stand up and say
three days later He arose and is still alive today?

This is what Jesus endured:
skin ripped off his back so that your soul would be assured.

To ensure you would be here on today.
Do not let another moment waste away.

Open up your mouth, spread the good news,
use every avenue He gave to you.

Someone is waiting, assigned to you.
Will a life be changed because of what you do?

Is it you that Zion is calling?

CHOSEN

Many are called,
few are chosen.
Where each man stands, only God knows it.
One called to witness,
another chosen to lead souls,
but only God knows.

To be your very best,
never fail God's jealousy test.
Stay in your lane;
pray others do the same;
together we can win this game.
Never covet another man's treasure;
you may never know his lack of pleasure.
Stay true to who God made you to be,
and don't try to be me.

Many are called,
few are chosen.
But to when and where
only God knows it.

LOVE

When my eyes met yours across the room
I could see the sparkle as you looked;
you smiled so gently, yet looked so deeply.
I know this was more than a common meeting.

As time would move, so would you;
showing me you cared in all you do.
Accepting all the time, just as I was
wrong or right, you proved your love.

Interference did come to drive us apart,
but interference could not steal what was in our hearts.
God by His power has made us whole;
there is so much more to this story yet to be told.
Every beat of our hearts has made a song;
a song of love that will forever sing on!

THE SOUND OF LOVE

Love sounds like your voice whispering in my ear,
saying "how I love you so dear."

Love sounds like a door through which everyday you walk
coming home to me.
Oh, yes I see.

Love sounds like your loyalty, which you give so freely
being so very faithful only to me.

Your love is so true
when I hear the words, "I only think of you."

Love to me sounds like the day you fell on one knee
and said, "Baby, marry me."

The sound of love is the steps we take;
hand-in-hand everyday.

Through good and bad,
we somehow make it last.

Love sounds like your arms wrapping around my waist;
your soft lips against my face.

This sound I hear when I'm with you
drowns out all other noise from breaking through.

Life seems to pause; problems go away;
all other issues take second place.

My mind slows down, my body is at rest;
In your arms is where I feel my best.

This sound I hear cannot be duplicated;
the sounds of two hearts becoming one
    man did not create!

There is nothing I have ever felt so strong.
How I feel when I'm in your arms,
    the gentle melody of a love song.

This sound I hear
was made by God only for my ear.

You are mine and I am yours;
let's make our sound of love forever more.

BABY BOY

Stomach aches, cramps, and pain.
What's the diagnoses? The doctor began to explain.

A few test results we await so we'll all know your fate.
A few moments more have passed away.

In comes the physician—
"I have good news," she says, as I hold my breath and
    await my disposition.

All tests have the same results:
"You're going to be a mommy in six months!"

My heart beat, my stomach sank.
This would be my first child. I don't know what to think.

Emotions run rapid.
        Hormones on a roll.
                Appetite increasing.
                        Wow, where did my waist go?

Pound for pound, my baby shows its size;
taking over my body like rain pouring down.
Wandering what it will be.

I'm counting the days as they lead into weeks;
the months stack as my baby grows inside of me.

Now moving from side to side;
flipping and flopping, This is now Mommy's pride.

Morning sickness is continual;
Weight gain is prominent,
  but what's growing inside is so valuable.

An ultrasound proves my greatest suspicion;
I'm getting what I have been wishing.

A bouncing baby boy.
            Soon to be in my arms;
                  he's going to steal my heart—
                        I can feel it.

Months have passed
and the news is a bit sad.

An emergency delivery is at hand.
This was not what I had imagined.

Into the hospital, on the bed,
epidural in my back,
"Oh no, I don't feel my legs."
A little while has passed.

Now, the Dr. says,
"We have him out," and places him in his dad's hands!
We both look as we cry.
We almost lost him, but thank God he didn't die.

Many accomplishments in life to proclaim,
but this is one, that, without shame,
I show to the world proudly everyday.
Mommy's baby boy;
my love, my joy!

As A Mother

The day I became a mother my life forever changed.
All that was about me had been reframed.

My son came into the world and it seemed as though
I was placed in the shadows, as he would grow.

Like a thief on the loose, he stole my heart
every chance he got right from the start.

Thinking of the time that he grew inside;
Makes me give God all of my worship
and lift my hands high.

God was kind and so good;
He blessed me to experience this kind
of love like a mother should.

Whatever the care or the need,
as a mother you have become my greatest priority.

As a mother my love he can feel and see,
I will live my life demonstrating the love of Jesus in me.

TIME

Time is an element that waits on no man; keep up
with him or get another plan. Don't mess around,
he won't wait for you — moving on and on, as
time will do. If by chance you miss your turn,
stay put for a while, your time will return.
Now once in hand do not waste him or
play around; too many others are
looking for him in this crowd.
Shoving and pushing, each
wants a turn to meet
Mr. Time and
be heard. Friends
become foes, lovers
become haters — all over
time commanding the other to be
patient knowing that his appearance is so
rare, use him wisely you may even share; but
whatever you do don't let him pass you by, and be
ready when you see him or say to Mr. Time goodbye.

As The Sun Sets

As the sun sets over the water
it takes my breath away.
So beautiful and serene, right here I could stay.
The wind blowing softly causes a gentle wave.
A few fish leaping . . . Toward the end of the day.
Tides are rolling in . . . sky's darkening.
I'm enjoying this view like an artist;
enjoying the silence that speaks in its own way.
Birds tweeting, preparing to take their rest for the day;
nature has a way of showing her best,
watching the lovely waves and a brilliant sunset.

CHANGES

Life has a way of changing who you are.
The life you have lived and known for so long
can be turned at the blinking of an eye.
Joy can be turned to sadness,
your laughter into a cry,
leaving you with one question . . . . "Why?"

Being rooted and grounded in this life means a lot.
Things can change, and then what?
One day can leave your life in complete disarray—
from one stable moment and suddenly drifting away.

One bad decision can cause ruin.
One wrong person in your life today
can lead to 18 years of regret and repay.

Many years you can reside behind prison doors
because of one outburst of anger;
one bullet out of control.

The way things were
before those life-changing moments can almost be a blur.
Getting back to normal is what most people desire.
But what is normal today
just might pass away.

How things used to be, the good old days.
Money in the bank, life going your way.
Relations great, children doing fine.
Business on top, and maybe a little reserve on the side.

But don't lose sight because of where you are;
tragedy may not be far.
Life-changing moments can occur
leaving you confused and unsure.

Use your tragedy to broaden your sight.
Don't make the same mistakes twice;
become a better person this time around at life.

Decide to do better and be better.
Decide to help your brother.
Allow character and integrity to have a place.

Do the right thing regardless of what people say.
A new normal may have to come into play, but
allow your life change to make you better today.

FEELINGS

How do I explain what I feel inside?
How can I continue to hide?

What I feel is so out of control.
What I feel is a pain from my soul.

So how can I console the agony of this cry
that seems to be so loved?
How can I cry so, and yet there is no sound?
This is a midnight cry; only He can hear from up above.

One that others may not hear.
And yet, the sound is so clear.

This is a cry from deep inside
that may not express tears to the naked eye.

Pain that may be felt for days and months to come;
one that cannot find comfort.
A midnight cry.

As I lay here on this bed,
When will I see the breaking of day?
When will this night pass away?

When can I smile and know that all is well?
When will I see the light of day begin to propel?

How much longer before this midnight will pass?
How long will I last?
Can my mind hold on through this maze of torment?
Will my inner being continue being silent?

The answer to the questions I ask may not be evident.
However, if I continue to hold on through the night,
there is a morning;
A sunshine that will give my soul a ray of light

FREE

It's time to let go
of all that has been
holding me down and
holding me back.
It's time to be free.

Free to soar,
free to create,
free to come into my destined place.

I want to be free.

Free to be you,
free to be me.
Come everyone,
Let's be free.

No longer held by shackles in my mind.
No longer having to hide.
No longer being afraid of success.

Let's be free.

Free to write.
Free to sing.
Free to build.
Free to live.

Just be free.

Let no hate control your actions.
Let no negative words create a pattern.
Let no mistake slow you down.
Let nothing in your past cause you to hold your head down.

Let's go. Let's soar.
Let's ride the waves of success.
Let you be you and me be me.
We have passed the test.

Let go of your fear.
Let go of the mess.
Let go of anyone that won't celebrate & elevate you.

It's time now to be free.
Free in your mind body, soul, and spirit;
free in every area.
Can you now feel it?

Be

No longer waiting for permission.
No longer needing approval.
Just be what the word is—

. Free.

Take a deep breath.
Inhale your freedom,
exhale your limitations
because this is our season.

Let's be free!

As I Lay

Here on my bed
unable to move.
So many questions.
Lord, what shall I do?

No movement in my legs;
no sound from my voice.
Thoughts running rampant;
spirit refusing to be torn apart.

As I lay, people in and out pray for me;
some stay.
Others lend a hand out
but are able to walk away.
But I can't move;
paralyzed from the trauma,
wishing he didn't make me
come back to this drama.

No promise from the M.D.
Just hang on in there as the days go by.
"We will see."

Holding on to my faith is what keeps my spirit high.
Knowing God has a plan for me, I know it's not my time to
die.

Speaking to my body with thoughts in my mind,
constantly quoting "I shall live and not die."
In this time of darkness the enemy comes,
no need to listen because he is the father of every lie.

But I am so glad I have the word of God hidden inside of me.
"Hide the word in your heart" is what Psalms reads,
and in a moment like this
it's surely what I need.

Not being able to read due to a blinded eye,
I have to rely on what was already inside.

The words I have studied,
the words I have preached,
the same words
I have taught
must now be walked out.

Would I stand and believe the words I know,
or would I give in to the enemy?

This is the moment
one's faith must come to life.
Do you believe God?
Is it for Him you live or die?

This is a time when my decision to believe should have been made long ago.
Thank God my soul does say "Yes," for when trials hit my soul had already been saved.

So on today not being sure of what tomorrow may throw,
be sure your anchor holds.
Have you received the Lord as your personal savior?
Have you said yes and not maybe?

On today make sure
you know where lies the eternity of your soul.
Make sure you have a firm grip
and REFUSE to let go.

BUT I'M STILL HERE

Feeling fine.
Looking good.
God supplied all my needs every time.

Doing God's will,
expecting nothing less.
When I asked, He always blessed.

Becoming ill or destitute was the last thing on my mind.
Why should I think of defeat
when I know God is on my side?

With a firm grip of God's word
my attitude was set.
I spoke against the enemy and will not be trapped in his net.

Although tests and trials
come to make us strong,
isn't it easier to tell all of them to move on?

Speaking faith is a tool we must use;
not being weak or timid,
for that's what your adversary expects of you.

Be strong in the Lord and in the power of His might.
Stand firm on His word
during the day and during the night.

Matters not what you may face.
Always remember
God's grace.

If he could not bring you through it
He would not
lead you to it.

So let the words of your mouth
and the meditations of your heart be acceptable in His sight.
You will win this fight.

For He is our strength and our Redeemer;
our guiding light.
I'm still here because of His words I remember.

ABILITY

With eyes to see I can view;
beholding all the possibilities
that I may choose.

With my ears to hear
I listen to the sound;

the sound of calm,
the sound of peace,
a sound from heaven—
just for me.

With my nose I sense a scent;
a smell so sweet drifting
with the wind, twirling
through the trees.

Roses and daisies,
Grass and leaves,
just to smell the scents—
what a relief!

Hands to write
and point if need be.

          Arms lifted for holding and hugging.
          Legs to walk, run, and dance.
          Feet that move in the direction at hand.

          How I've learned to appreciate
            the smallest to the greatest;
        grateful for movement and ability.
               I thank God daily.

Until you have been in a paralyzed state—
no movement or feeling but believing by faith—
you can't understand how precious ability can be.

              What a joy;
              What a relief!

A zest for life;
an excitement of expectancy;
a pure and distinct directive;
a delight for life daily.

In using every muscle available,
these all refill my life now that I am able.

Yes, I am able—to bring hope to this world
by proving that God is more than a fable.

Every part of me is a testimony,
and with this life I will keep on running.

SURVIVOR

A survivor is what I am;
to be sick as I was, yet healed as I am.

A survivor is who I will be;
telling people all over of God's grace and mercy.

Standing at death's door on one afternoon;
now I stand well, full of life right before you.

God was not done doing his work through me;
He was not done showing how powerful He could be.

At the moment my enemy
thought he had gotten the best of me;
God showed up, rebuked the enemy,
and caused many to see.

To see that healing is the children's bread;
He brought me back, I am no longer dead.

A child of God I am born again and
covered in His blood I stand.

Healed and set free from infirmity and disease;
now I am going to fulfill my destiny!

THIS TIME

A second chance at life is not often granted.
A second chance to live one more time;
an opportunity to make wrongs right;
a chance to get involved and win this fight.

This time will be different, just wait and see.
The mistakes of yesterday won't hinder me.
Don't try and block me; that won't work.
Don't try and stop me as
I advance God's Word.
Advancing forward is my goal;
taking back the life the enemy thought he stole,
and making every minute of each day
a moment to remember; no time to delay.

This time life has meaning that can't be explained;
a thrust forward that won't be chained.
So now, an announcement as I shout to the world:

THIS TIME I STEP FORWARD AS A BRAND NEW GIRL!

THANKS

A few words of thanks as I think of God's good grace.
A few words of thanks when I see your face.

For the times my body lay lifeless,
needing lotion or a cool wiping—

Thanks.

For rubbing my head in my deepest despair,
for hearing your voice and knowing you were there—

Thanks.

For filling my feeding tube with food to eat,
for putting socks on my cold feet—

Thanks.

For helping me up and sitting me down,
for turning me over and turning me around—

Thanks.

From one doctor to the next,
making sure they were the best—

Thanks.

Therapy days and brain tests.
Yes, those seasons were a mess—

but Thanks.

From bed to chair to walker I progressed.
You pushed me around like a child in distress—

Thanks.

This thanks is to you on today
you gave me your best, and for that I will love you always.

Thanks.

CONCLUSION: HIS GIFT

Salvation is a gift that comes
   from God our Savior.
He made it available to you and I
   because we are in His favor.

I know this to be true
   because He did it for me.
Open up your heart,
   and He will allow your eyes to see.

That He is the Answer,
   the Truth and the Light;
the only way to get to God
   is through Jesus Christ.

This gift is not about material things,
   although He gives them to us.
This gift is about being reassured that,
   in Him, you can trust.

You can trust that He will do
  exactly what He said He will.
He will bless with the gift of health
  so you no longer have to take pills.

He is a Healer indeed,
  but that is not all;
He conquered death and gave us life,
  and now your name He calls.

Calling on your heart
  so you can reign with Him in the conclusion of life.
He gave you free choice,
  but choose Him and there will be no remorse.

The conclusion is simple,
  but are you ready for His truth?
Confess with your mouth,
  believe in your heart, and cut the devil loose.

Romans chapter 10, verse 9
  gives you the outline for salvation.
Read the Bible about His gift,
  and your conclusion will help save nations.

THE
SOUL JOURNEY
CONTINUES...

ABOUT THE AUTHOR

Prophetess Tronotia Balka is a trusted voice in the Kingdom of God. Through her amazing testimony, lives are being transformed and souls are being welcomed into The Kingdom. She is now broadcasting live every Tuesday at 3PM on *Blog Talk Radio*. Her show is called *The Prophetically Speaking Radio Show*. Prophetess Balka also has an upcoming television talk show, which will be aired on the UHN Network in the Spring of 2015. It will be broadcast in Houston, Texas, as well as over the Internet to the rest of the world.

God is truly using Prophetess Balka's prophetic voice to set the captives free. Not only does God speaking through her for the radio and national television, but also through her writing as well.

Prophetess Tronotia Balka's list of books include:

- 10 Hours Later (Fall 2014)
- A Prophet's Prayer Journal (Spring 2015)
- The Power of Me (Fall 2014)

The above listed books are only a few of the prolific writings that God has released through Prophetess Tronotia Balka. Along with her ministry efforts, Prophetess Balka is the mother of one son, Roy, whom she adores. She is the proud Daughter of Reverend Davis Malveauex and Minister Nellie Malveauex. As a family that stands on God's word, they are certainly a force to be reckoned with.

Prophetess Tronotia Balka is an active laborer at The Harvest Time Evangelistic Church located in Houston, Texas, for which Bishop Shelton Bady is the Pastor.

Jeremiah 1:1-10 and Isaiah 61 are the scriptural bases of this prophetic movement.

This is the hour...

Now is the time...

YOUR PROPHETIC DESTINY IS AT HAND!

NEED A MINISTRY SPEAKER?

TB Ministries

Your Prophetic Destiny is at Hand!

Prophetess Tronotia L. Balka is a Christian ministry speaker, author, and entrepreneur who has engaged the body of Christ and compelled unbelievers about the amazing love of God for over 20 years.

Recently, she has been lead of God to travel the world testifying of her death, her experiences in Heaven, her journey back to life, and her massive recovery. God graced her with His miraculous healing.

Prophetess Balka's powerful testimony is just a snippet of her ministry abilities. She is anointed with a powerful prophetic mantel to teach the word of God in a way that captures the attention of those who hear her.

Speaking engagement requests and bookings may be done on her ministry website tbministries.net . Kindly complete the "Book Us" form and provide detailed information about your event. Prophetess Balka or someone from her ministry will contact you within 3 business days. Thank you.

Stay in Touch

Stay in touch with Prophetess Tronotia Balka and TB Ministries by visiting the following websites:

TB Ministries Website: TBMinistries.net

Radio Broadcast:

blogtalkradio.com/TBMinistries

Facebook:

facebook.com/pages/TBMinistries/455601081183624?ref=br_tf

Twitter:

Follow #TBMinistriesA or go to twitter.com/TBMinistriesA

Don't Forget Your

Additional Resources

Thank you *Soul Journey* Readers, I am ever so grateful that you have chosen to read my book!

I, and those of us here at TB Ministries, pray that you have received a God-anointed impartation into your life through this book and our ministry.

We believe that this book is a great resource to help encourage and inspire you through any type of situation. We also believe that although our book, and those like it, can be of great use, the Holy

Bible is the ultimate resource and guide for every question in life. Please, seek out a Bible and a Bible teaching church near you that will be able to further help guide you on your *Soul Journey*.

As a "thank you" for picking up a copy of the book, I'd like to invite you to visit my website (tbministries.net) for free resources and ministry insight to assist you along your journey.

www.ingramcontent.com/pod-product-compliance
Lightning Source LLC
Chambersburg PA
CBHW031526040426
42445CB00009B/417